Live L-I-V-E!

LIVING A LIFE OF ACCOMPLISHMENTS IN THE FACE OF OBSTACLES

Keeler Bryson

Vision Writers Publishing, LLC
Sherwood, AR

Keeler Bryson - Vision Writers Publishing, LLC
P.O. Box 6516
Sherwood, AR 72124
www.KeelerBryson.com

Live L-I-V-E! - How To Live A Life Of Accomplishments
Keeler Bryson —1st ed.
ISBN 978-0692336120
0692336125

Contents

Dedication

I dedicate this book to those who are trying to accomplish something noteworthy, but keep getting side tracked by the obstacles of life.

I dedicate this book to those who have lost their zeal for life, due to the obstacles of life.

I dedicate this book to those who have become champions at living L-I-V-E! in spite of their obstacles, the odds, their dysfunctional upbringing, the negative words and lies spoken over their lives.

I dedicate this book to those who have helped me in some way, whether good or bad, to now live a life of accomplishments! To God Be The Glory!

Live **L-I-V-E!**

—KEELER BRYSON

Introduction

Since I wrote my first book, my life has been activated in a way I use to dream about. I'm amazed at how God can place assignments within us that we didn't know we could accomplish. But then, at the right time, He will activate that gift/assignment in our life, calling it forth into the atmosphere!

My first book has gone to countries I haven't traveled to yet. I'm thankful for those I do know who purchased my book and I'm amazed by the fact that people I don't even know felt led to purchase my book! This is nothing but the favor and amazing grace of God; to Him be all glory and honor! And so here I am again releasing another book into the Earth realm. I'm not sure how many books I have down inside me, but one thing's for sure, however many God has ordained me to write, they shall be written!

Over the years, I've had many experiences. Some were good and some not so much. I've always been a deep thinker regarding life, its lessons and the wisdoms that can be gained from it. Life is a mystery. How we think and the decisions we make each day determine the quality of life we'll have. I believe most of us want to live the good life, but struggle with how to manifest it, especially if we've come from backgrounds of struggle and dysfunction. Thus, most of us are doing some sort of activity we believe will lead us to the good life. Some get married, some attend college, some join churches, some pursue being a professional athlete or musical artist, entrepreneur, etc. We do these things hoping they will yield to us the good life we desire. But the truth of the matter is, after most of us have done all of the above things, sometimes we still find ourselves without the intended result. We then become discouraged and depressed with our life.

In order to possess the life God designed for us, we must keep ourselves focused, motivated and activated. We do this by being exposed to real life changing information, healthy relationships and power charged atmospheres that feed our God designed life. If we don't feed the seeds of destiny, purpose and potential that God planted within us, those seeds will die. And we will feel like "the walking dead," mainly because our spirit is longing to live the life God designed for us to live. I believe many of the unhappy folks, whether they realize it or not, are unhappy because they're not living the good life God designed for them to live. It's a miserable feeling to wake up each day with the potential and ability to be a world changer, but end up hanging out idle and unproductive each and every day. Most people believe that as long as they are "good" each day, God will be pleased with that, not realizing that we are going to have to give an account to God for our wasted time and/or unproductive life.

God has always burdened me with doing what I could to help encourage, inspire and motivate others to see and release their potential. I truly love being an encourager and motivator. That being said, one day I had a dream and in the dream God showed me a sign that said, "Live L-I-V-E!" When I saw the sign in the dream, I felt its power. When I woke up, I began to meditate on what God had showed me, because I had been seeking Him for a slogan for my Monday night motivational conference call. When I saw this sign, I knew God was showing me what my slogan or mantra should be.

Live L-I-V-E! is only two words, but very powerful. God wants us to do two things: 1. Live and 2. Live L-I-V-E! Do you know that it is extremely hard for many to do these two simple words? Go to the grocery store, work, church, family gatherings and just watch people's faces, words and actions. You will see a lot of folks who are not living L-I-V-E.

People seem to be wandering, confused, angry, mean and hateful and some do this all in the name of Jesus! I believe most people who demonstrate the afore-mentioned behaviors do so because they're not living a Live L-I-V-E! life. If you are reading this book, you're about to read some thought provoking sub-jects on how to Live L-I-V-E!, which will lead to a life of fulfillment and accomplishments. In this book I will cover several thought provoking topics that will challenge, encourage, guide and activate you to begin your journey towards living a life of accom-plishments, as designed by God. If we can just begin to continuously execute these simple changes in our daily lives, these changes will lead us to living a L-I-V-E life! If we're going to Live L-I-V-E,! we must be a committed doer of the directions that will lead us there.

As you read through this book, let the words soak and simmer in your spirit. Really take the time to think, meditate and answer the questions that are asked. Examine your life as you read through the pages. Besides, aren't you tired of always reading good information, getting inspired and then nothing permanently ends up changing in your life for the better? If this is you, then keep reading and let this book teach you how to move from residing in the same old place career wise, emotionally, spiritually, financially, mentally and physically, etc. and move towards the Live L-I-V-E! life God has in mind for each of us!

A Life of Accomplishments

There are many ways to living a life of accomplishments and many desire living a life which has something to show for the time spent here on Earth. It's a sad thing to have been given the gift of life and do nothing with it. The accomplishments we achieve are payments for the air we breathe. I believe each of us possess the ability to live a life of accomplishments. I believe that just as God expected those in the Parable of the Talents in Matthew 25:14-30 to earn a profit on what they'd been given, so it is with each of us. God expects us to make a profit on the life, talents and abilities He's given us.

Many have been fooled into believing that because of their mistakes, limited resources, poverty, lack of education, dysfunctional upbringing, color, gender, etc, that they are unable and incapable of accomplishing any successes. However, I'm a witness that, if you have a **strong desire** to accomplish some successes and defy the odds, you can, with the help of God! If you "will" to do it, you "will" do it!

Looking back at my childhood and at the hand I'd been dealt, the statistics said I should have gotten pregnant at a young age, dropped out of school, be unmarried, living in poverty, strung out on drugs and alcohol, been to jail, lazy, unproductive, ignorant, etc. I remember when I was in junior high school, evidently, one of my teachers recommended me for the Peer Facilitator Program for at risk students. Basically, they tagged me as being "at risk." I assume this was because I was a Black female teenager from a single female parent home. Back then I didn't realize the implication of this, but as I got older and began looking back at how far God had brought me, I saw God's hand on my life even through this program.

You see God was protecting and expanding me via this program. I didn't feel I was at risk, but based upon the statistics of the hand I had been dealt, I was at risk, or so they thought. Later on, I was recommended by a teacher to be a tutor at this same junior high school. I was smart you see. At any rate, I agreed to tutor students who were struggling with math, reading, etc. And the school district paid me. I laugh at this now, while feeling a sense of pride at the same time. Again, I saw the hand of God on me in this situation too. He was revealing to me, even then, that I was born to teach and get paid for it! To this day, I teach people how to get what they want and how to live the life they want. I love learning and teaching!

At each pivotal moment of my life, God always had someone placed in the right place at the right time that would assist and/or guide me to the next step or phase of my life. I remember reading Ebony and Jet magazines when I was young and I would see African-Americans in there who had earned their Master's degrees in Business Administration. This inspired me so much. A picture of their success showed me a picture of my potential successes. This created a desire in me to get my MBA, even though at the time I really didn't know what it meant to have an MBA. It just sounded good and I desired it! These people looked successful. They looked like they were accomplishing their dreams and goals. I wanted this too. Years later, God granted me my heart's desire!

Conversely, not only did God use situations like this to inspire me to be an achiever, He also used the naysayers. For example, I started working for the VA Medical Center, part-time, while in high school via the COE Program. And after graduation, they allowed me to continue to work there because I was attending college.

Keep in mind that I got married 90 days after my high school graduation, started college full-time that Fall and then two years later, I had my first child. I did all this while working part-time for the VA Medical Center.

Well, one day while I was at work, they had a reception for all of the COE students. They had cake and punch and they took a group picture of us. Everything was going well, until the program director decided to come and chat with me. She found out I was married, had a baby, attending college full-time and was working there part-time. She wanted to know how in the world I was going to "accomplish" all these responsibilities.

I guess I was so ambitious, until I hadn't realized the load I was carrying, until she made it a point to bring this to my attention. I felt like I could do it and I didn't see any reasons why I couldn't. Her attitude towards me was mean spirited. The enemy was attempting to use her to release a quitting spirit on me. She was trying to snatch away my confidence/faith in my ability to accomplish all that I had on my plate. But thank God I had joined the Church in high school, was full of the Holy Ghost and had developed a level of faith and spiritual warfare ability!

Otherwise, she probably would have gotten to me that day. The tone in which she spoke to me was very negative and it hurt me so bad! I was thinking to myself, she's supposed to be an encourager to the young people she was in charge of. Her job was to cheer and support us, not kill our dreams and ambitions or spew her negativity and doubt on us. I had to fight back my tears, but at the same time I was angry! I was like how is she going to project her own inabilities and weakness on me? Evidently she couldn't see herself doing what I was doing and felt the need to shift that mind-set onto me. But all she did was prophesy to me!

That day, I learned that whenever a superior attempts to tell you what you are incapable of doing, take this as a Prophetic Word that God is going to do that exact thing in your life! And He's going to get the Glory from it too! Not only did I earn my undergraduate degree, with honors, I earned my graduate degree, with honors. I've been with the same man for 25 years and I have successfully raised my first child! I did just what she said I couldn't do! BOOM!!

What am I saying? I'm saying that God has a plan for your life. He has given you the ability to manifest your desires in spite of the opposition and in spite of the odds that are stacked against you. I believe there are some unleashed accomplishments inside of you that are waiting to burst forth. Now realize there will be challenging and difficult moments on your journey towards accomplishments, but just know that this is apart of the process. So don't let it stop you!

If you will trust, depend and obey God, He'll lead you to your desired destination. I wrote this book for people who desire to be better and have a better life, but can't quite figure out how to accomplish this desire. The formula is simple, but sometimes we make it hard. Sadly, as a result, many get distracted and never complete their journey to an accomplished life. Don't let this be you.

Whatever accomplishments you achieve in your life, it is at that moment you will have broken the cycle of that particular generational curse off your life and bloodline. What a powerful thing! I've been able to break some generational curses off of my life, as a result of my accomplishments. Let me teach you how to do the same in your life.

CHAPTER ONE

Where Are You?

We live in a culture that has so much GPS tracking technology until there's no excuse for being lost. We have MapQuest, Google Maps, Scout Maps, etc. These devices are designed to get us to our destination, without getting lost.

All we have to do is simply enter the start address and ending address. And from there, the device will map out a route for us, tells us how many miles it's going to take in order to arrive, as well as how long it will take to arrive there. What's really neat about some of these devices is that some of them will actually **speak the directions** to you! What's interesting about this process is that we trust the directions we're given. We actually go where the voice system tells us to go, without any hesitation or distrust. If we follow the directions, eventually we arrive at our destination.

When you look at your life right now, where are you? Have you entered the start and end address for your life? Are you in route to your preordained life? Are you lost? Do me a favor, think back on last week. What did you do with your moments and hours last week? Did you sleep most of the week? Did you spend most of that time texting, talking on the phone to friends, on Facebook, Instagram, Twitter, watching TV, etc.? Did you spend most of last week working? Or did you spend last week stuck in the depression of a breakup?

If we rarely take time to ask ourselves, "Where Am I?" we'll never arrive at our preordained purpose.

And we'll be driving around in circles, going no-where. If we don't know where we are, we don't know whether we're offcourse or on course to our destination. **Whatever we're doing each day is either taking us towards our preordained purpose or moving us away from it.** The purpose of this passage is:

- To make you think about whether where you are right now is where you should be at this moment in time

-Is where you are right now a healthy place?

-If it's not, what do you need to do to change this?

If you're lost or need better directions for your life, here's what you need to do in order to move towards your preordained purpose:

-Before you go to bed each night, write out your agenda for the next day.

-Map out how much time you will spend on each item.

- Get up a little earlier for meditation/prayer/guidance.

- Read something inspirational each morning.

- View your vision board.

- Speak positive affirmations over your life and goals.

- Avoid negative influences that try to tempt you in the wrong direction.

- Repeat, Repeat, Repeat.

CHAPTER TWO

How to Start Living Your Purpose

If you really want to live and experience the life God purposed for you, you've got to take charge of your life, be careful who you listen to and finally, you've got to step out in Faith at the leading of God. A few days ago, I achieved another major accomplishment, as a result of a previous accomplishment. You see, one accomplishment leads to another one. At any rate, I have been totally amazed at what God has done in my life these past six months!

He's done more in my life these past eight months than the past five years, all because I stepped out in Faith. I realize none of my accomplishments would have happened if I had not completed some corresponding faith actions that were in alignment with what God desired to accomplish in my life.

The first action I took was to take charge of my life! Yes, I became unapologetic about "**my** life focus." I did this by deleting and discontinuing any and everything that did not support or accommodate what I was endeavoring to achieve. This is very important! I began to take inventory of my life in order to determine what was actually bringing value and/or increase to my life. I identified people and things that I felt was slowing me down and/or the cause of me not being authentically me. God can't bless who you pretend to be. I began to examine relationships, teachings and the belief systems I'd been taught. What I found was that many of my relationships were not adding value or increase to my life. In fact, some of them were subtracting from my life "frequently," causing frustration, stress and sadness.

I further realized that many of my childhood teachings and a certain amount of my religious teachings were not as necessary, accurate and effective as I was led to believe.

As a result of all these enslavements, God had to really do a great renewing of my mind these past five years in order for me to "Live L-I-V-E!" His purposes for my life. Be mindful, however, that it takes A LOT of courage to do this step because when you do it, many will not understand what you're doing and will become upset and disappointed with you. But I must remind you that **this is your life**, so take charge of it! If you live a "people pleasing" and "religious people pleasing" life, you won't achieve God's purpose for your life because God can't use a person who's MORE in love with pleasing people and religious institutions than pleasing Him. When you do this, you'll find your life in the same place and miserable, year after year. So take charge of **your** life!

After all, it's the only way you're going to start living your purpose.

The next step I took was, I became selective in who I listened to. At a conference I recently attended, one of the speakers said, "Never take lessons from a coach who never played the game." This statement was so profound to me because there are a lot of people acting like a coach, giving lessons/advice about a game they've never played. You definitely cannot listen to these type of folks, because they will mess your life up by getting you off course to fulfilling your purpose, as a result of their bad coaching/advice. They will tell you that you shouldn't do this or that. They'll tell you this or that won't work, etc., etc., etc.! They'll even have you believing that you can't achieve your purpose without them. Some will even try to intimidate you with their position of authority. **BEWARE, THIS IS NOT OF GOD!**

Here's one way I've learned to discern good advice: Ask yourself whether the person giving you advice have already lived it and/or possess what it is you're trying to achieve? If not, you may want to seek advice from a person who does. One thing I've grown frustrated with is people who are giving advice that doesn't work! You never see the fruit of what you were advised to do. And if you continue to listen to them, the more you will get brainwashed to believe their bad advice. I've found that a lot of people are giving out advice that they received down through the generations. It hasn't proved to work and everyone knows it. But because it's tradition to keep passing along the bad advice, no one has the courage to question or challenge the advice, out of fear of being reprimanded or labeled abominable. It's time out for repeatedly doing unproductive things! This is the definition of insanity. Be careful of listening to people who claim to be experts, anointed, educated, etc., but don't have the proof/fruit to support their advice. Anything successful and blessed of God reflects visible, exponential GROWTH!

The final step I had to take is, I had to step out in Faith. I had to get to a point where I no longer thought about what I wanted to do, prayed about what I wanted to do or continue talking about what I wanted to do. I had to step out in Faith and TAKE ACTION! towards what I wanted to achieve. Many get stuck at this step. I admit this step is uncomfortable and scary, but it's necessary! Stepping out in Faith is how we get God to intervene Supernaturally into our situations and aspirations.

Many believe in God and are faithful to their religious organizations and routines, but when it comes to stepping out in Faith, these same individuals are paralyzed with fear like a deer caught in headlights.

In your pursuit of fulfilling your purpose, God will sometimes give you some instructions that are not logical, but if you will follow/obey them, God will show you His power in ways you never experienced before! If you will step out in Faith, a Supernatural force will come upon your situation/life that will take you out of "time" and leap you years ahead of where it otherwise would have taken you five to ten years or more to accomplish! And you will look back and be in awe at how you achieved what you did in such a short period of time. All God need is for you to do these three things consistently, so He can demonstrate His power through YOU! in the Earth mightily in these last days! Will you be one of the ones He can use?

CHAPTER THREE

Being Authentically You

W hen we look around society these days, we see few individuals who are authentically being the person God created them to be. We have so many copy cats. And it's been said that with each additional copy, of a copy, a certain amount of resolution is lost. Bluntly stated, we have too many folks mimicking others and not displaying their own authenticity. There's entirely too much duplication going on! I believe we were born with the right and freedom to stand out....to be different. God wants us to be different. However, many institutions would like, and sometimes demand for us to think alike, dress alike, live alike and learn alike.

We must remember and/or realize that it's okay to be authentically you! Authentically you, whereby defining and expressing your own style, preferences, beauty and life. Look around. Even the Universe itself is a testament that God wants us to be different. Otherwise, He would have made us and everything else look the same.

Many of us have decided to "fit in" with the status quo, at the expense of losing our own authenticity. And as a result, when you ask most folks, "Tell me about yourself or Who are you?" They are stunned at the question and find it difficult to articulate who they are because sadly, they don't know. For years, they've lived their lives according to the opinions and influences of others. And when we do this, we end up not knowing who you we and we don't know what we want. I have found that when most folks are asked who they are, they give off generic answers that everyone is accustomed to hearing.

Their answer is very superficial. But I want to challenge you to BE AUTHENTICALLY YOU! Get off the bus of going along to get along!

So what does "authentic" mean? Not false or copied; genuine; real; honest. So if you're not being authentic, you're being false, copied, not genuine, honest or REAL. You're a pretender....an actor....a fake. When you're not authentic, the "real" you can't come forth because you're busy being someone or something fake. If you're not being authentically you, you're wasting precious "life" time....you're wasting time in this life being someone else and not who God designed you to be.

When you decide to start being who God created you to be, you will find the real you. Life will be so much easier and better. You will begin to live in freedom because you're no longer masking yourself or your true feelings. You will be happier and will live a happier life. When you're not being your authentic self, it's like living life in bond-age/slavery, because you wake up each day living life the way society (peers, TV, culture, social media, religious institutions, etc.) says you should live.

Signs You're Living A Life of Inauthenticity:

1. Your Voice: When we're not being ourselves, we tend to use a high voice. We're not projecting from our belly and chances are everything below the neck is starved of breath. Or you may be talking superfast. These are signs of discomfort, due to inauthenticity.

2. Your Body: Are you clenching your butt, hands or jaw? Our bodies have billions of cells firing all at once and those cells can't be fooled. Tension in your "being" is picked up instantly by your body. This too is a sign of inauthenticity.

3. Your Breathing: Shallow breathing in the chest area vs. the belly will not only change your voice, it's also a signal of fear, nervousness and inauthenticity.

4. Are you in the present moment or are you being hyper-vigilant? When we're feeling safe and authentically in the moment, we relax and respond naturally. When we're not, we're hyper-vigilant, watching others for signs that we're being accepted, liked and believed.

Ways to Create an Authentic Life:

1. Redefine Your Values. It's hard to behave in an authentic way, if you do not know what you value and desire. Often, we hold tight to the same values we grew up with, when we need to reevaluate what feels right to us. We must get clear on what we care about. This will allow authenticity to kick in.

2.   Have An Open Mind. Authenticity flourishes when we experience life with an open mind and from every perspective. Rigid, good/bad thinking keeps us trapped in judgment and limitation, which causes us to shut down our vulnerable, authentic self. Challenge yourself to **look at all sides of a situation.** Be open. This is one area that's difficult to do, if you're super religious. Super religious people tend to live a life of inauthenticity via masks and facades. Thus, preventing them from living a life of authenticity.

3. Notice When You Are Being Inauthentic. To do this, you must pay attention to those times when you are insincere in your speech, or when you are acting in a way that doesn't align with your core values. Then explore the fears and beliefs that may be causing barriers to your authenticity.

4. Trust Your Intuition. We tend to feel out of sync, when we are acting inauthentic. We don't feel right

when this happens. When this happens, this is your instincts telling you that you are not being genuine and that you're acting a lie. At this point, bring yourself back in sync with acting authentically. This will prevent you from getting trapped in an inauthentic life.

CHAPTER FOUR

Don't Drift in Neutral Any Longer

A re you drifting in neutral? Does it seem there is no particular destination for your life? Most of us at some point in our lives have wondered what is God's plan for our life. At times, we feel we know God's plan for our life and then at other times, we don't. As a result, we find ourselves drifting in neutral. When this happens, we tend to feel lost and hopeless. I have found that an unexpected loss or tragedy has the capability of snatching us from a place of directional "know how" into a state of drifting. Far too many times the tragedies of life prevent us from getting into "drive." Depression, alcoholism, drug use, quitting and giving up are examples of drifting in neutral. When we're drifting in neutral, we lose our vision. Proverbs 29:18 says, "Where there is no vision, the people perish." Having the wrong vision with regard to our lives, is also a contributing factor to drifting in neutral.

To drift means to be carried slowly by a current of air, water or force of circumstance. It means to float and wander. Antonyms of drift are: fly and speed. In other words, when we're drifting, we're not controlling the direction of where we're going. Outside forces are in control. This means there's a great possibility we may end up somewhere we never intended to go. When we're drifting, we're moving "slowly" in the same place. As a result, we're not making progress. Neutral means to be out of gear, to deviate from a set course. If you've ever driven on ice before, you know the effects of the neutral gear. You're neither in reverse or drive. You're in a gear that's designed to slow the car down, ultimately causing the car to come to a stop. Wow! Think about that. Drifting in neutral will slow your progress down and eventually stop you. You are unable to drive forward or in reverse. You're stuck.

How Does One End Up "Drifting in Neutral?

-Their Thoughts (negative thoughts; no vision)

-Their Belief System (improper teaching)

-Fear

-By Choice

How Do You Know Whether You're Drifting in Neutral?

-You're still in the same place you were last year

-You can't identify anything you've accomplished that you're proud of

-You feel lost, unfulfilled and apathetic

How Do We Stop Drifting in Neutral?

-Read & Meditate Jeremiah 29:11

-Decide Where You Want To Go/Accomplish In Your Life (SEE IT)

-Research/Map Out How To Get There

-Count Up The Cost

-Get in Drive & GO!

Assignment: Put together a Vision Board for yourself. A Vision Board is a board that you place pictures and words on that reflect what you desire in your life. Search for examples on the internet. When you're done with your vision board, post it up somewhere in your house or office where you can look at it each day to remind yourself what your vision is for your life, thereby shifting you from drifting in neutral and into drive.

CHAPTER FIVE

Being Wise With Your Resources

When we are resourceful, God will send us more resources. Being resourceful produces increase because we become even more gifted with the ability to stretch, save and sustain our resources. When we're resourceful, we are creative. When we're resourceful, we create something out of nothing and more out of less, with leftovers.

To be wise means to be intelligent, cleaver, witty, prudent and judicious. A resource can be your time, income, possessions, wealth, property, goods, supplies and stuff. These are the things God wants us to be wise with using. To be wise is to be resourceful. Being resourceful is the ability to use what you have in order to reach a desire or need.

Biblical Examples Of Resourcefulness:

- Gideon in using the jars and trumpets (Judges 7:16)
- Jesus feeding of the 5,000 (Matt. 14:13-21)
- Elisha and the Widow's Oil (II Kings 4: 1-7)
- Samson using foxes, torches and the jawbone of a donkey (Judges 15:3-5;14-16)
- Ruth demonstrated resourcefulness in picking up the dropped corn after it had been harvested (Ruth 2)

Biblical Examples Of Those Who Were Not Wise With Their Resources:

- The Prodigal Son did not demonstrate re-sourcefulness, but wasted his inher-itance (Luke 15:11-32)
- The Foolish Servant buried his talent and ended up losing even that (Matt. 25:14-30)

Are you wasteful? Are you resourceful? Here are some tips on how to be wise with your resources:

- Plan - do something each day that will help your future
- Buy Smart – purchase items when they're on sale, buy in bulk i.e. tissue, paper towels, light bulbs, etc.
- Reuse – buy short-term use items and non-essential items at second hand stores i.e. clothes for growing children, tools, books, etc.

- Borrow – for items you rarely need or use, borrow from friends, family & neighbors
- Share – if you or someone you know have more than enough of an item to share, do so
- Fix & Maintain – instead of buying a new car, washer or dryer when it breaks down, find out how much it would cost to repair these items. Many times it's more cost effective to repair vs. making a new purchase.

CHAPTER SIX

Are You Happy?

A t this very moment, Are You Happy? I mean really and truly happy? If so, good for you! If not, why are you not happy? What needs to be done in order for you to live happy daily?

It's no secret that I love Pharrell Williams' song "Happy" from the movie Despicable Me 2. It doesn't matter what I'm doing or how I'm feeling, when I hear this song, it brings my "Happy" out in a BIG way! And from what I've seen in the media, I'm not the only one who loves this song! People from all over the world have been uploading videos of themselves singing and dancing to this song. I believe the reason this song has been so popular is because it ministers to us and reminds us that happiness is a choice. In fact, if you listen closely to this song, it provides the remedy for unhappiness.

The first thing I noticed from this song is that Pharrell starts off by noticing how the Sun is shining. I tell my friends and clients all the time that, as long as I see that the Sun did rise that day, I know everything is and will be alright! So the first step in gaining and maintaining your happiness is to look around at the elements. If you see that the Sun rose, there's oxygen in the atmosphere, the birds are singing, etc., this is your sign that God is still in charge. Since He's making sure the Universe is operating properly each day, then He'll do the same for us. This is something to be happy about.

Secondly, the song instructs us to clap our hands. In other words, get your praise on. Throw your own praise party. Turn on some "happy" music! In spite of how low you may be feeling, find a song that will lift your spirit and begin giving God praise for the things that you are grateful for. For it's been said, "When we pray, God releases Angels, but when we praise, God comes Himself!" So if you really want a shift in your situation, start praising God! You will find yourself feeling so much better.

Finally, the song declares victory, in spite of any bad news. We must do what the song says and declare we're going to be just fine. We must declare to whatever trouble we're going through that it's wasting it's time and that we're not going to let nothing bring us down, because our level is too high! Get your happy level up! Because if you sit down and really think about it, you have too much that's going well in your life to be walking around unhappy.

Stop counting your problems and start counting your blessings! It may sound crazy to do these steps when you're in the midst of a heated trail, but I strongly challenge you to do these steps anyway. Scripture says that when Paul and Silas where in prison, they found the fortitude to give God the praise in spite of their predicament. And as a result, the Power of God showed up on their behalf and Supernaturally released them from prison. I believe we can become so happy until whatever had us bound emotionally, mentally, etc. will loose us and let us go! Bob Marley said it best, Don't Worry, BE HAPPY!

CHAPTER SEVEN

Operating In A Spirit of Excellence

2014 has been a very, very busy year for me. As I sit here reflecting on this year, there are several powerful moments I experienced, but the one that stands out the most was a great opportunity that was offered to me, as a result of my operating in a spirit of excellence. If you are desiring greater opportunities, I encourage you to be committed to operating in a spirit of continual excellence in all that you do!

To operate in a spirit of excellence requires excellence to be a part of your entire being...your mind, body and soul. It's who you are at your core.

Excellence is the quality of being outstanding and extremely good. Excellence is the setting of high standards, a state of excelling; superiority and eminence. Far too many times, we witness folks who are not operating in a spirit of excellence. If you're like me, it is very irritating when this happens. I'm sure you have witnessed being serviced by someone who just didn't give a hoot about the quality of work they were doing for you.

In addition, they probably had the attitude that they were doing you some sort of great favor that you should be grateful for. Service like this, regrettably, is now an all too common example of deteriorating customer service across the country. Whether you're working on your job, in your home, at school, church or in your community, always do it in a spirit of excellence.

The great blessings and great doors of opportunity you desire are reserved only for those who possess and operate in a spirit of excellence, which in the end brings glory to God. God is elevating those whose work has been branded with the spirit of excellence!

Whether you realize it or not, you are a brand. Your brand is a representation of what you believe and care about. It's up to you whether your brand will be recognized, respected and properly compensated. Some of the most expensive products available are expensive because its creator has a reputation of providing superior, high quality products. People will pay for excellence!

For years I've always endeavored to operate in a spirit of excellence. My mom raised me this way. While endeavoring to do an excellent job in whatever I was called, assigned or hired to do, there

Have been times when those around me would get irritated with me for operating in a spirit of excellence. They would tell me I was too persnickety, acting like I was OCD and that it didn't take all that because no one is perfect. I know they meant well, but excellence is who I am and I just can't allow my work to fall below the standard of excellence. Be warned, operating in a spirit of excellence will bring criticism and opposition. However, I am committed to excellence.

For years it seemed my meticulous efforts were in vain, but I kept at it. Little did I know, but God was teaching me discipline in operating in the spirit of excellence so that once He opened the great door of opportunity for me, I would already be effectively trained and prepared to serve people with authority and influence. Quite frankly people of this caliber don't want just any old body to serve them. When you operate in a spirit of excellence,   people you don't even know will know you and will respect you and the brand of excellence that you've established. My question to those of your reading this book is, "What are people getting when they get you?" Are they getting superior quality or junk? If you want to get noticed, promoted and paid, endeavor to operate in a spirit of excellence. God is looking for qualified candidates to promote.

If you want God to open great doors for you, decide to rise above the rest. Let God train, develop and refine your gifts and talents, via the discipline of operating in a spirit of excellence, so He can present you before Kings and Queens. If you are diligent in your work and committed to operating in a spirit of excellence God will recognize you, honor you and compensate you accordingly.

CHAPTER EIGHT

The Power of Focus

There is power in being able to focus. And in order to achieve anything worthwhile, it will require focus. Being focused is work. Being focused is a learned art and once you master it, you will experience the power of it. This power is exhilarating!

For many, focus is hard to do because you have to be persistent and consistent in working towards your goal, even during distractions. Distraction is one of the number one reasons many fail at achieving their goals because they are unable to remain focused during distractions. In many cases, if these individuals would simply become relentless in their focus, they'd achieve their goals.

All that I've ever accomplished: a great marriage & family, college degrees, career in real estate, owning my own businesses and becoming a self-published author all were accomplished as a result of FOCUS, in spite of the distractions and setbacks.

I was determined to achieve success in each of these areas. When you really want something bad enough, you will give all your focus to it. If you struggle with staying focused, I suggest that you invest in a life coach to assist you in developing your focus and holding you accountable, so you can achieve your goals. Once you see the return on this investment, you'll be glad you made the investment in yourself!

Focus is disciplining your mind and actions in order to fulfill a goal or dream. No dream or goal is achieved without focus, but with focus anything is achievable. As we enter a new year, I challenge you to become more focused so that you too can experience the power of focus!

CHAPTER NINE

Transitioning to Due Season

Often, just before we enter our "due season," we experience a "dry season." Transitioning to our due season is no easy task. During the dry season of the transition, it is sometimes tempting to become discouraged and give up. But Scripture says, "for in due season we shall reap." The condition, however, is: "if we faint not." This passage is for those who are on verge of entering their due season, but feel faint, weak and weary. To you I say, "Be not dismayed." What you're currently experiencing is a normal part of the process of transitioning to your due season. Transition is the process or period of changing from one state or condition to another. In life we will experience many transitions. Some transitions are easy, others are painful. In order to successfully transition through painful, dry seasons to due seasons, we must first define a dry season. This will help us to better understand where we are in the transition process, so that we won't faint.

A dry season is a season where it seems nothing is working out like it used to. It's a season where we will experience rejection and an unusual amount of toiling and exhaustion in an attempt to get things to work out like they used to. A dry season is a time whereby old methods and experiences no longer provide the effectiveness and solutions it once did. A dry season is an announcement that it's time to move up to the next phase/level in order to accomplish a greater preordained purpose.

For example, in Scripture Peter and his partners had been fishing all night and caught nothing. Keep in mind that these were experienced fisherman who made their living by fishing. These were fisherman who had fished this particular area successfully several times before, but during this particular fishing trip, they had "toiled" all night and caught nothing. As a result, they finally made up their minds to wash their nets and go home. Their circumstance had to be extremely overwhelming, because not catching any fish would affect them financially. All the investment they made that night to catch fish did not yield their desired return. All the time and energy they had exerted produced nothing! This had to be frustrating!

Many times when we're in transition to our due season, just like Peter and his partners, we too will feel like we've done all we know to do, based upon our past successes, but yet see no return on our investment. We followed the same formula that worked before. We even went above and beyond the call of duty in many cases, yet we find ourselves at a loss for words to describe the dry place we've found ourselves in. Being in a dry place can be down right mind boggling. We know something is wrong, but we can't quite figure out what or why. However, I've learned over the years that when we don't know what to do, we have to open ourselves up to God for an answer and then He will step in and help us! You may be tempted to be mad or upset with God because you're in a dry season. But never get so mad with Him that you become too stubborn to invite Him into your dry season. This is an isolation tactic of the enemy.

Scripture says Jesus came to Peter and his partners and told them to launch out into the "deep" and drop their nets (plural). But Peter, who was probably feeling irritated and tired at this point, told Jesus that they had already been toiling all night and caught nothing. But nonetheless he obeyed Jesus' instruction. We must do the same no matter how ridiculous God's instructions may seem to us, especially after we've already tried several times. Peter, however, partially obeyed Jesus' instructions because Scripture says when he dropped his net (singular), he caught so much fish that his net almost broke from large amount of fish he caught.

As a result of following Jesus' instruction, Peter and his partners went from a dry season into their due season. In their dry season, they had to toil all night. In their due season, they simply had to obey Jesus' instruction. They had to be willing to humble themselves and put their fishing expertise aside and try Jesus' new way of fishing instead. Once they did this, they caught a slew of fish and they didn't have to toil for it! Obeying a simple instruction, in their moment of frustration, transitioned these men into their destiny as well. Their destiny/purpose was to become fishers of men by working in Jesus' ministry. A dry season can sometimes lead us to our purpose and destiny, if we don't over ride it.

Once we enter our due season, we become endowed with Supernatural ability to accomplish MORE doing Less! Once we enter our due season, our dry season is dismissed and we begin to encounter a mighty breakthrough that releases a harvest on a level we've never reaped on before! Once we enter due season, there will be new opportunities, new and better methods revealed, new strength, new lessons to learn, etc.

So remember the next time you find yourself in a dry season, rejoice! For a dry season is an announcement that you have outgrown your current season and it's no longer sufficient for you. It's an announcement that you're about to go to a higher level of living and serving. The transition to your due season may be uncomfortable, overwhelming and exhausting at first, but you shall reap it, if you faint not!

CHAPTER TEN

Overcoming the Spirit of Panic

P anic is defined as a sudden overwhelming **fear**, with or without cause, that produces hysterical or irrational behavior, and that often spreads quickly through a group of persons or animals. When someone is experiencing the spirit of panic, it will cause them to lose self-control and partake in frantic actions that they would otherwise not do, if they were not panicking. The spirit of panic is also known as panic attacks. According to statistics, at least 20% of adult Americans, or about 60 million people, will suffer from panic attacks at some point in their lives. Symptoms of a panic attack usually begin abruptly and include rapid heartbeat, chest sensations, shortness of breath, dizziness, tingling, and severe anxiousness. To the point, panic attacks stem from fear.

With such diversities of disaster, compounding challenges and overt opposition being felt by many these days, it's become imperative more than ever for us to guard against the spirit of panic. In the Scripture, when the children of Israel were at the Red Sea, and saw that Pharaoh was coming after them, after he had let them go, they began to panic. The spirit of panic began to spread throughout their camp. Scripture says they began to cry out to the Lord. They began to speak frantically. And lastly, they began to attack and blame Moses for what they thought would soon be their demise.

The children of Israel had a history of reacting this way each time they were confronted with an opportunity for progress. If we're going to advance in

God and possess the blessings of God, we must learn how to overcome the spirit of panic! Life is filled with challenges and many of those challenges can be frightening, but we must "know" our God. If we know our God, we shall do exploits! The way we get to know Him, during our times of challenge, is by trusting Him and allowing His rescue plan to manifest in our lives, instead of running away in panic and fear.

Trusting Him means having confidence that He will deliver us, assist us and provide for us. Trusting Him means not blaming Him or reneging on our commitment to Him. Truth be told, many curse God when it appears He's not coming to their rescue during a challenging moment. Trials and tribulation have a way of showing us where we are and where we are not in God. It was obvious the children of Israel did not know their God because if they did know Him, they would have reacted better.

They were on the verge of another Supernatural manifestation, but was overcome with the spirit of panic.

It's important to note that the spirit of panic shows up right before we're about to experience the Supernatural power of God. When it does, it will have you thinking you should go back to the place where God delivered you from. The spirit of panic will have you thinking that you were better off in Egypt (sin & bondage). In fact, many do go back to "Egypt" because they were consumed with the spirit of panic. The spirit of panic will cause you to believe you have no better options, but this is a lie!

Lastly, the spirit of panic will cause you to think and act out extremely irrationally. Fortunately, Moses was on the scene to coach the children of Israel out of the spirit of panic!

Here's what he told them and it's still a Word to the wise today.

1. Do not be afraid.
2. Stand still.
3. See the Salvation of the Lord.
4. Make Declarative Statements.

When overcoming the spirit of panic, we must first calm down, take authority over our fear. We must SPEAK what Scriptures have said about fear. One of my favorite Scriptures about fear is found in Revelation 21:8. It says, "The fearful and unbelieving would go to the lake of fire." Wow! Did you feel that...how this Scripture snatches out fear? I call this a "Snatching Scripture!" It's powerful! It's evident that God doesn't tolerate fearful people! In fact, He considers it sin. DO NOT BE AFRAID!

Secondly, we must stand still. This means stop and slow down. It also means to stop allowing our emotions, cynical words and thoughts from running wild all over the place. Put a halt to this behavior immediately!

Thirdly, we must "see" God. We must "see" ourselves in victory. We must get a better vision (God's vision) of our situation, instead of a vision of demise and defeat. We do this by looking at our situation with our spiritual eyes. We must see God's provision coming to assist us.

Finally, we must declare the victory regarding our situation. We must "say something" (something good)! Moses did and God did just what Moses declared. Fear not, for the Lord is with thee!

CHAPTER ELEVEN

Getting Your Plans To Succeed

What are your plans? Have/are you experiencing any success with your plans so far this year? Why or Why not? In order to achieve anything of significance, effective planning is needed. The trick to fulfilling our plans, is having the right plan. This requires seeking the advice of an expert, especially when treading new territory, ideas and projects. Without expert advice, our plans risk unforeseen failure. I believe very few people are intentionally planning to fail. However, if we fail to plan, we plan to fail. Most of us want our plans to succeed. We desire a successful career, marriage, family, finances, business, etc., but what do we need to do in order to succeed in each of these areas? When we have an important dream, goal or assignment before us, it can be very overwhelming at times, because we don't always know how to get the plans done, who to trust, who to contact and most of all, we don't want to fail.

I want to suggest to you that, God is a trusted, all knowing Source, who knows the secrets of success. He knows the paths we should take. He knows the paths we should avoid. He knows which connections and partnerships would be most favorable and beneficial to us. He knows which job we should pursue and accept. He knows where the jobs are, where the funds we need are. He knows what we should do, when we don't know or are confused about what we should do. God is a Strategist! He's full of wisdom! He's the Master of Success!

Sometimes we get so caught up in making our plans, that we error by not making God our Business Partner/Adviser. Because we're not conferring with God, with regard to our plans, we end up not having success. God wants our plans to succeed, but they won't succeed, if we don't meet with and discuss with Him the best approach to getting our plans to succeed. We can avoid a whole lot of pain and misery, if we would simply tap into the wisdom of God, the Master Planner.

When we commune with God, He will show us and reveal to us the hidden secrets of success. And it won't take us years to fulfill our plans either. He knows the short cuts to success. He knows how to get things done, without the money we thought would be needed. If we would simply and consistently "sync up" with God, our plans will manifest and succeed. His advice is tried and true. He has unconventional ways of enabling our plans and dreams to succeed, if we will commit them to Him.

Proverbs 16:3 says, "Commit to the LORD whatever you do, and your plans will succeed." (NIV) To commit our plans to the Lord means to: **transfer** our burden to the Lord and cast upon him ALL that we have to do. As a child **opens his heart** to a tender parent, so should we show to God our desires and intentions, **trusting** His care and providence. And then **our thoughts will be established** and **we'll meet with a happy fulfillment**, because our plans were undertaken, according to the will of God, and directed to the end, by His guidance.

We don't have to carry the burden of successfully manifesting our plans alone. When we commit our plans to the Lord, we roll the burden that comes with that plan, over to the Lord. Because some times our plans can become too heavy to bear/fulfill alone, thereby imploring us to get help. If we are going to get our plans to succeed, we must refer all our actions and concerns to God and then depend upon God's providence and grace for assistance and success. This is how we get our plans to succeed!

LIVE L-I-V-E! | 79

CHAPTER TWELVE

Live Outside the Box

In this passage, I challenge you to live outside the box! I want you to know that you don't have to live your life like everyone else. You don't have to do "it" like everyone else is doing "it." Look around, most of the people you see who are living inside the box are stuck, trapped, limited, suffocating and miserable. Living inside the box is congested, jam-packed and full to capacity.

Living inside the box limits your ability, creativity, finances and freedom. This is because in order to live inside the box, along with everyone else, you have to live your life just like everyone that's inside the box. And if you don't, those who are in side of the box will criticize you, terrorize you and eventually disconnect from you.

What Does Living Outside the Box Mean?

- To Think For Yourself
- To Live A Life That's Not Based on The Opinion of Others
- You're Not Afraid To Be Different - Most of life's greatest accomplishments are achieved by people who break the mold.
- You're Open To New Ideas & Possibilities
- To Break Free From The Status Quo
- To Reject The Nonsense/Lies/Manipulation/ Control
- To Take A Stand!
- To Speak Up!
- To Make Unpopular Decisions

How To Know Whether You Are You Living Inside A Box:

- You feel trapped in a life that's based upon the beliefs of someone else
- You desire to make changes, but are afraid of what others will think
- You're Broke
- You find yourself always acting in accordance with the beliefs of the group/persons you're with at the time, as if you believe the same way, but privately, you express your feelings of disagreement
- You're always going along with what others say and believe in order to avoid conflict
- You feel unhappy
- You're having health problems
- You feel you're living a lie/double life
- You feel you're just existing and not living
- You feel there's more to life than what you're currently experiencing

- You feel all the rules, opinions and beliefs you've been taught and have followed, have not produced the results you were taught
- You feel like you're missing out on "life" because you're living inside the box

How To Live Outside the Box:

- Identify areas where you're living inside the box
- Ask/Discover why did you allowed yourself to live inside the box in the first place
- Troubleshoot how to address possible back-lashes/attacks that could happen as a result of you deciding to start living outside the box
- Decide what you need to do in order live outside the box
- Do It!...Start Living Outside the Box!

- When "second guess thoughts/people" come to try and talk you out of getting out of the box, remember your "why" and don't turn back

The Materials of Great Accomplishment

*"Obstacles Are The Raw Materials of
GREAT Accomplishment."*
-Tommy Newberry

In closing, one thing that I know for sure is that life is **full** of obstacles. And although we'd like to avoid them, the truth is, they are the building blocks of great accomplishments. This means there's no way around them, if we're going to accomplish anything noteworthy. Therefore, we've got to become a people who are champions at living L-I-V-E! in spite of the obstacles, our dysfunctional upbringing, negative words and lies spoken over our lives. We must get to a point where we learn to accept, embrace and overcome our obstacles. Because right behind the obstacle, is the prize.

Most of the lessons in this book were written as a result of various times in my life when I was facing my own obstacles, while attempting to accomplish my personal dreams and aspirations. I followed the tips in this book and they brought me to the finish line! I trust, believe and pray they will do the same for you.

If you will remember the lessons in this book and utilize the tips that were provided, you will be better equipped to handle obstacles when they show up in your life.

No matter what obstacles you may find yourself facing, remember there is one thing worse than dealing with your obstacle and that is not living L-I-V-E! When God made you, He had a purpose in mind. That purpose was planted within you long before you arrived on Earth. And now your entire life's assignment is to discover that purpose and fulfill it. In doing so, you will not only Live L-I-V-E! but you will live a life of **great accomplishments!**

About the Author

Keeler Bryson is a Teacher, Motivational Speaker, Life Coach and Author. She holds a Bachelor's of Arts degree in Organizational Management, a Master's degree in Business Administration and a Ph.D. in Overcoming a Hard-Knock-Life. She is the founder of Teachable Life Moments, LLC and Vision Writers Publishing, LLC.

She is the author of the book, <u>Crisis Management: How To Manage Personal Life Crises</u> a book she was inspired to write as a result of repeated, overwhelming, devastation in her life. In the book she coaches the reader through the process of personal life crises by sharing personal crises she's experienced and the principles that helped her emerge from them successfully. After becoming an experienced crisis overcomer, Keeler now lives with a passion to encourage, equip and inspire others to be overcomers so that they can fulfill their purpose.

She's happily married to Grover Bryson for over 20 years. They have two daughters, Whitney and Miracle.

I Want To Hear From You!

If this book has inspired or helped you in any way,

write me or email me and share your story.

Teachable Life Moments, LLC
P.O. Box 6516
Sherwood, AR 72124

Email: Keeler@KeelerBryson.com
Website: www.KeelerBryson.com
Twitter: @KeelerSavant